Introduction:

Many people know Aberystwyth as a  ersity own, and an important centre of We 'hich punches above its weight', and has to, ?as, surrounded by vast areas of very sparsel ...interland. Far fewer have sampled the delights of ...interland on foot, and hopefully this book will serve as an introduction to visitors who would like a detailed guide to shorter, half-day excursions.

Visiting walkers are amazed at the superb and unspoiled scenery on offer, and wonder why they didn't try it out sooner. The proximity of the National Parks to the north and south mean that you leave the crowds behind here...paths are well waymarked yet small and unworn, and you will find coast, mountains and deep forested valleys abounding with wildlife rather than people. Spot the numerous red kite that were rescued from UK extinction right here, the buzzards and ravens, and the famous winter 'murmerations' of starlings that roost under the pier. You might even catch a glimpse of the very rare pine marten, a stoatlike mammal, amid the remaining ancient sessile oak forests of the Rheidol valley. The area is noted for its clean, clear air and water, mild winters and (for Wales) its relatively lower rainfall and more sunshine hours.

This is hill country...even on the coastal path! So if you have done little hill walking a few words of advice are necessary. In the unlikely event of an accident, help will take much longer to arrive than in a town, so it is important to be well enough equipped to avoid the slip in the first place. Some paths are steep and slippery, and walking boots with thick socks are needed to maintain safety and comfort. It also does rain, so good waterproofs are essential all the year round! The nature of the terrain makes it difficult to give precise timings for walks...they depend so much on walking rates and weather conditions.

At this point it is only fair to add that although the authors have researched and checked every walk as carefully as possible, of course you proceed entirely at your own risk...Fencing, gates, stiles and landscape features are constantly changing, and you should feel comfortable in your ability to follow your route on the OS map as well as using the small maps in this book.

There are numerous walks in the Rheidol Valley, served by the Vale of Rheidol narrow gauge steam railway. Only two are described in this book, but for the many others, please see the sister publication, 'Railway Walks in the Vale of Rheidol', by Maurice Kyle, available at the Tourist Information Centre, and the Vale of Rheidol railway shop in Park Avenue.

Distances

The length of each walk is given in kilometres (km) and miles.

In the walk descriptions there are instructions such as "in 500 m the lane crosses the ....." to help you to follow the route. If you are not comfortable with metres (m), then such instructions can be read as 500 yards or 500 long paces, as these distances are only an approximate guide.

Maps

It is highly recommended that you use OS 1:25 000 Explorer maps in conjunction with this book. 17 of the walks are on map 213 Aberystwyth and Cwm Rheidol. 3 walks (8, 9, and 11) are on map OL23 Cadair Idris and Llyn Tegid, and walk 10 is on both 213 and OL23.

All the maps in this book are orientated with North at the top.

N
↑

Gates and stiles

See the note on page 9

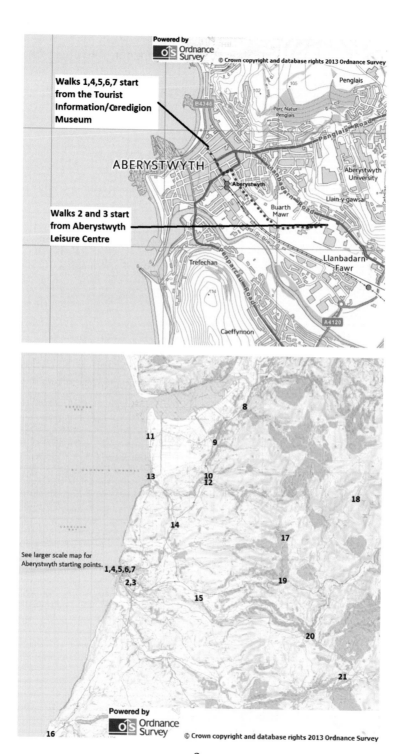

Walks 1,4,5,6,7 start from the Tourist Information/Ceredigion Museum

Walks 2 and 3 start from Aberystwyth Leisure Centre

See larger scale map for Aberystwyth starting points.

Contents, walks in the book.

Walk No.	Description	Starting Point	Category	Distance km (miles)	See page number:
1	Aberystwyth and Constitution Hill	Tourist Information Centre	Easy	6.5 (4)	6
2.	Aberystwyth, University Campus, Parc Natur Penglais (Penglais Woods)	Leisure Centre	Moderate	6 (4)	10
3.	Aberystwyth, Llanbadarn Church, Frongog, and Comins Coch	Leisure Centre	Moderate	7 (4.5)	16
4	Aberystwyth, the Harbour and Pen Dinas	Tourist Information Centre	Easy	6.5 (4)	21
5.	Aberystwyth, the Harbour and Tanybwlch Beach	Tourist Information Centre	Easy	9 (6)	26
6.	The Ceredigion Coastal path: Tanybwlch, Allt Wen and Morfa Bychan	Tourist Information Centre	Hard	13 (8)	30
7.	Aberystwyth Town Trail	Tourist Information Centre	Easy	4 (2.5)	33
8.	Furnace, Artist's Valley, and views of the Dyfi Estuary.	Furnace village (bus or car)	Moderate	5.5 (3.5)	41
9.	Tre'r- ddol and Cwm Cletwr	Tre'r ddol village (bus or car)	Moderate	7 (4.5)	45
10.	Talybont and Bedd Taliesin	Talybont village (bus or car)	Moderate	7.5 (5)	49
11.	Dyfi National Nature Reserve, Ynyslas dunes and Afon Leri boatyard	Ynyslas Turn (bus or car)	Easy	5 (3)	52
12.	Linear walk from Talybont to Borth.	Talybont village (bus or car)	Moderate	6.5 (4)	55

No.	Description	Location	Difficulty	Distance	Page
13.	Linear walk from Borth to Aberystwyth	Borth lifeboat station	Hard	9 (5.5)	58
14.	Rhydypennau and Llandre Circular.	Bow Street village	Easy	7 (4.5)	62
15.	Linear walk from Capel Bangor to Aberystwyth (via steam railway)	Capel Bangor Station	Moderate	8 (5)	65
16.	Llanon to Llanrhystud Linear Coastal Walk	Llanon village	Easy	4 (2.5)	68
17.	Craig y Pistyll Gorge and Llyn Syfydrin	Llyn Pendam car park	Hard	8 (5)	71
18.	Ascent of Pumlumon Fawr via Maesnant	Maesnant	Hard	7.5 (4.5)	75
19.	Bwlch Nant-yr-arian Visitor Centre; Circular via Llechwedd Gwinau	Bwlch Nant-yr-arian	Easy/Moderate	6 (4)	80
20.	A railway walk; Devil's Bridge to Rhiwfron Halt	Devil's Bridge station	Easy/Moderate	3 (2)	83
21.	A gorge walk at the Hafod estate	Hafod Estate top car park	Moderate	5 (3)	86

Walk 1: Aberystwyth and Constitution Hill   Easy

6.5 km (4 miles), about 2½ hours. Starting point: Tourist Information Centre
Grid ref. SN584818

No visit to Aberystwyth is complete without ascending Constitution Hill and en-joying the classic views of "the Biarritz of Wales" and Cardigan Bay. This circular walk passes Penglais Nature Park, Aberystwyth Golf Course and overlooks the Clarach Valley before ascending Constitution Hill from the North. The route uses well-signed paths, tracks and lanes through the town, open countryside and woods.

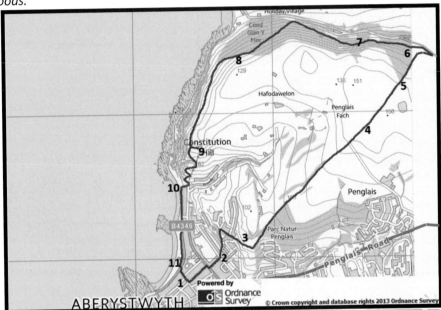

1. Leaving the Information Centre in Terrace Road, turn left and immediate-ly left again into Portland Street, at the end of which can be seen the Town Library (ex Town Hall). At the end of Portland Street, cross Queen's Road to stand in front of the library. Turn right and then immediately left to walk to the top of Loveden Road. Cross North Road, and on the opposite side, look for the sign for Gelli Anwen.

6

2. Ascend Gelli Anwen, which includes a long flight of steps, until you emerge on Heol y Bryn. To your left are the offices of the Welsh Books Council. Cross Heol y Bryn, turn right and after passing Pen y Graig on your left, you will shortly see a gap in the hedge, giving access to Penglais Nature Park.

left. Cross the field to a stile. In the second field keep the fence on your left. Pass through a metal gate and in the third field keep the hedge on your right until you come to a facing stile and 5-bar wooden gate. You have now completed the first ascent and are entering Cwm Woods.

3. Follow the track gently uphill until a view of Aberystwyth appears on your right. Continue on the track, ascending a small flight of steps, and after a level stretch, pass through a gap and go ahead with a stone wall on your right. After reading the warning about golf balls, follow the path uphill between the right hand stone wall and Aberystwyth golf course on your left. After nearly 1 km you will reach a gate leading onto a broader rough track. Turn right and follow the broad track for about 200 m to where it turns left; your route is straight on through a metal gate into a field.

4. At this point there are the ruins of wartime buildings on your right and

5. In the woods follow the path downhill for about 250 m where it starts to turn right. You will shortly see a road ahead. Immediately before the road, turn left on a signed path.

6. Follow this path through the woods. After about ¾ km of gentle ascent you will see a protective metal fence on your right and a little further on you will meet a lane. Views to the right are of the valley of the River Clarach.

7. Walk down the lane until it takes a hairpin bend to the right. Your route is straight on uphill through the conifers. Passing through a gap in a fence, continue uphill to reach a gate after about 400 m. Passing through the gate turn right and follow the fence, on your right, down to another gate* which leads on to the coast path.

see footnote about gates and stiles

8. Turn left and follow the coast path uphill to Constitution Hill. Leave the coast path to visit the welcoming Consti Restaurant, the Camera Obscura,

and the summit station of Aberystwyth Cliff Railway (1896).

9. After you have enjoyed the classic views of Aberystwyth and Cardigan Bay rejoin the coast path (unless you

wish to descend on the funicular railway [in season]). The path shortly crosses a bridge to the left hand side of the railway and then crosses a second bridge to the right hand side of the railway. Complete the descent with care and emerge by the bottom station. Turn right and descend to the promenade where you may feel that you have earned the right to "kick the bar" (see the adjacent information board).

10. Turn left and walk along the promenade until you reach the bandstand (rebuilt in 2016).

11. Turn left and use the pedestrian crossing to reach Terrace Road and return to the information centre.

*gates and stiles

Ceredigion County Council are improving access by replacing stiles with gates where appropriate. Stiles mentioned in the text may have become gates during the lifetime of this book.

e.g. This is the stile that was previously at point 8.

Walk 2: Aberystwyth, University Campus, Parc Natur Penglais (Penglais Woods), the 'quarry path'.   Moderate

6 km (4 miles), up to 2 hours. Starting point: Aberystwyth Leisure Centre.

Grid ref. SN59481

A very varied and interesting circular walk close to the town, including beautiful woods and truly stunning high level views of the sea and town. The route is entirely on good paths and lanes, and the occasional route-finding difficulties are more than made up for by the quality of the walk. There are a couple of moderate ascents but no stiles to climb.

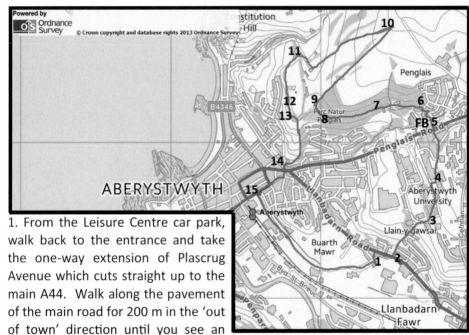

1. From the Leisure Centre car park, walk back to the entrance and take the one-way extension of Plascrug Avenue which cuts straight up to the main A44. Walk along the pavement of the main road for 200 m in the 'out of town' direction until you see an iron 'kissing gate' on the other side of the road, level with the house called 'Broadway'.

2. From here, follow a steep tarmac path which ascends straight up the hill alongside back gardens; where it meets a junction of paths go right then immediately left keeping to the uphill option. After about 300 m of this path you emerge onto a University campus

road on your left.

3. Cross the road onto a straight path which at first goes alongside the road, then cuts the corner off heading straight towards the Aberystwyth Arts Centre, with its neighbouring distinctive modern bell tower.

A short walk alongside the main campus road brings you to the flight of steps up to the piazza in front of the Arts Centre main entrance, alongside the Students' Union building. It is well worth a visit to the excellent Arts Centre, which serves the town and county as well as the University, as there are year-round exhibitions, performances, talks, classes and films.

4. From here, bear over to the left on the path between the Hugh Owen Library and the Arts Centre, emerging among the backdoor services, but then picking up the campus road which leads past the BBC building to the right, then the School of Education on the left. At this point, take the left fork, then follow the path squeezing through, alongside a hall of residence, eventually arriving at a long footbridge (FB) over Penglais Road, the main

A487. Crossing the bridge gives you your first lovely view of the town and sea, but there is much better to come!

5. After the footbridge, you are in the 'student village' (Pentre Jane Morgan) with its network of paths and roads.

Turn left in front of the nameplate and follow the concrete path downhill towards the next blocks of student flats, where you turn right immediately in front of them. Cutting through left,

then turning right on the road uphill slightly, you will see the exit from the village into the woods over on your left.

6. Following the woodland track for 150 m, arrive at a house on the right, where you bear steeply downhill left for a short distance on a stony path. This meets a wider path which you fol-

low bearing right, keeping on this past the Vice-Chancellor's house down to your left, and approaching the entrance to Parc Natur Penglais (Penglais Nature Park).

7. Pass through into the Park, where in May you will be rewarded by the sight of wonderful carpets of bluebells, but at any time of year, these woods are enchanting and rich in wildlife, with plenty of benches available to rest and enjoy the atmosphere!

8. Where the path opens out into a semi-clearing under a ring of majestic trees, turn right, and head uphill slightly until you come to a squeeze-stile across a dry stone wall. If you have trouble with this, there is an easier

way onto the golf course path by continuing a little further on the main woods path, then cutting back right next to the side gate to the golf club house.

10. Eventually, the path emerges onto a wider track quite high up on the golf course. Here, turn sharp left to face down the track, with a wonderful view

9. Turn right following the narrow path alongside the golf course, leading uphill for 700 m.

of the sea, and on a clear day, the coastline of Cardigan Bay running south as far as Cardigan Island. Walk down the track for about 650 m, taking in the marvellous views all round, until it meets the tarmac lane which leads to the golf clubhouse on your left.

Turn right downhill, walking past the council nurseries on the left, and the house set back called Plas Bryn-y-mor on the right. Here branch left on a stony track which ascends to a path crossing point with signpost, where you go left following the 'Penglais' direction indicated.

through the old quarry, now full of gorse bushes, then eventually you will arrive at a marvellous viewpoint, where there is a seat for you to have a rest and savour the fine view across the town and Cardigan Bay, and try to puzzle over the features artistically indicated on the viewpoint boards.

11. Follow this wonderful high level path winding its way along the bottom edge of the golf course, and then above the very northerly-most part of the town, with Pen-y-Graig below and Constitution Hill over to the right.

13. From the viewpoint, the obvious path ascends a series of wooden steps heading back up towards Penglais woods, but here go right instead on the smaller path, heading downhill, but then making sure to turn LEFT where it meets a T-junction of paths. Go right again very soon, descending rustic steps downhill, and continue downhill, meeting a larger path coming in from the left until eventually you come to the back fences of a row of houses, and then a gate leading out onto the bottom of Infirmary Road.

12. There is a winding section with steps where the path descends

14

14. Turn left into North Road, then cross busy Northgate Street, and into Pound Place, alongside the Coopers pub on the corner. Turn first right into Poplar Row, following this until it emerges into Alexandra Road, with the clocktower of the station straight ahead.

15. At the roundabout, go through the gates into the car-free Plascrug Avenue, and have a pleasant final 1 km stroll through to the Leisure Centre car park, just beyond the town rugby club.

Walk 3: Aberystwyth, Llanbadarn Church, Frongog, and Comins Coch.

Moderate

7 km (4.5 miles), 1-2 hours. Starting Point: Aberystwyth Leisure Centre.

Grid ref. SN594812

This walk is mostly along marked paths, surfaced tracks and lanes on the fringes of the town, with lovely views of the lower Rheidol valley and the surrounding countryside. The route is well waymarked and is easy undulating walking, but there are numerous stiles to cross. The walk includes a visit to the ancient and beautiful Llanbadarn Church.

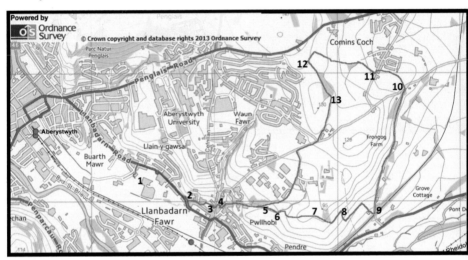

1. From the Leisure Centre car park, walk back to the entrance and take the one-way extension of Plascrug Avenue which cuts straight up to the main A44. There is a pavement along this section of the main road along which you walk in a direction away from town for 400 m, keeping straight on where the main traffic veers round to the right.

2. Ahead is the grey solid-looking Norman-style church with castellated tower. Go through the gate into the church grounds, and enter the impressive and beautiful building via the imposing porch. There had been im-

ortant early Christian buildings and a urrounding settlement here, much re-dating the town and castle, since he sixth century, if not earlier, but the resent building dates from the 13th entury and has been much renovated t various periods since. There is an xcellent exhibition in the south tran-ept detailing the history of the hurch.

4. This path is paved and pleasant, weaving between house gardens and crossing a footbridge before emerging onto a small back lane, still in the village, where you turn left up the hill. Pass the gates of the former primary school and continue straight uphill with the tarmac track narrowing and rising up into the woods.

rom the church, continue along the athway to the far gate, and emerge in he village square by the Black Lion nd Gogerddan Arms pubs. Turn left n the road here...be careful, this is ften busy with traffic.... and at about 0 m spot a gap leading to a public ootpath on the right immediately fter the last house.

5. There is a post to mark the end of vehicular access, and very soon after, spot a stile on your right. Cross the stile, and continue on a narrow path, a bit boggy after rain, which rises gently alongside a meadow with ponies, through a pedestrian gate and small bridge to the edge of an open green pasture rising ahead of you.

6. A waymark post indicates that you should turn to the left here, alongside the edge of the field towards a gate, then through the gate another waymark arrow points the way to the right, curving uphill alongside the field boundary. From this hill, a nice view gradually comes into sight to the right down towards the Afon Rheidol, and the twin bridges carrying the Vale of Rheidol Railway, and a pedestrian walkway. Behind is a good retrospective of the walk so far with the church tower, and the town and sea beyond.

7. At the top of the hill, go over the high stile into a broad pony field, spotting the footpath in the distance continuing between wooden fences,

about half way along the far field boundary. Cross the middle of the pony field, through the gate and into the edge of a copse, following the clear path which begins to descend with views between the trees to the right.

8. Over yet another stile, the way edges the field boundary downhill with the Glanyrafon Industrial Estate dead ahead in the valley below. But then a stile steers you left again, with wider views of the lower Rheidol valley, then turn right towards farm buildings lower down. Passing through three more gates you finally emerge onto a tarmac lane; locally known as 'Conker Lane'.

9. Here you are just above a bridge and cutting of the main Aberstwyth-

hrewsbury rail line...turn left uphill and walk for just over a km on this very pleasant narrow lane. With excellent views to the right, you pass the entrance to Plas Frongog, then the gradient levelling off past Frongog arm, before you arrive at a busier lane and an obvious footpath with 'kissing gate' continuing across the other side of the road.

11. Over this stile, head north-west across the hump of the field towards a stile in the far bottom corner. This takes you onto a surfaced footpath leading up to the row of cottages of Waun Gau, and beyond them, nearly to the main road... A487. Be sure to notice the view opening out behind you...with the sharply dipping dark hump of Pen Craig-y-Pistyll the most obvious distant feature, and far beyond, the smooth, gently-curved ridge of Pumlumon Fawr at 752 m.

10. This path curves round to the left uphill between hedges towards the village of Comins Coch, and arrives at another busy lane, where you turn left and walk for nearly 50 m until you spot a tiny, obscure stile almost hidden over the other side of the road.

12. Just as the track turns right to head up to the main road, cross the rather worn-out stile on the left into the pony field, and walk along the edge of the field, heading towards

the obvious gate and stile in the other field corner. Over this, continue on a boggy track through a copse which, after much slipping and sliding, opens out onto a grassy knoll, an excellent spot to admire the view of the distant hills. This is a remnant of the original 'red common' which gave 'Comins Coch' its name. There is also a disused quarry here, which no doubt helped supply the rougher shale blocks to build the older cottages in the village.

13. Continuing through a gate and stile, the track is easy to follow, emerging at a road junction which is very busy at rush hours. Heading in the same direction, cross the road and walk along it downhill on the pavement for about 200 m until you get to a narrow surfaced lane turning

off to the left. Follow this and descend past the Lluest Equine Centre where you keep straight on, not curving right. Eventually, after a pleasant easy walk you arrive back at the post in the track where you were earlier, after leaving Llanbadarn village.

14. Retrace your steps to the Leisure Centre by following Numbers 5-. above in reverse order.

TERRY 97

Walk 4: Aberystwyth, the Harbour and Pen Dinas.   Easy

.5 km (4 miles) 2 to 2.5 hours. Starting point: Grid ref. SN584818

*tarting and finishing at the Tourist Information Centre, this walk offers wonder-
ul panoramic views of the town, coast and sea from the hilltop Iron Age fort of
'en Dinas, with its iconic Wellington monument. The route is paved and fairly
!vel along Aberystwyth promenade and by the harbour, then on a small ascend-
ig path on Pen Dinas which can be muddy. There are no stiles.*

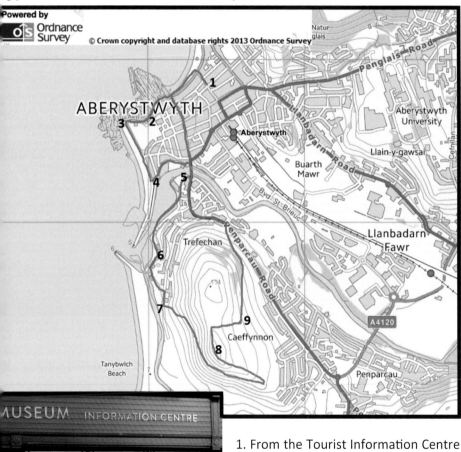

Powered by
Ordnance Survey
© Crown copyright and database rights 2013 Ordnance Survey

1. From the Tourist Information Centre in Terrace Road, head towards the sea-front and turn left along the prome-nade of Marine Terrace, passing the pier, which was the first in Wales, built in 1865.

2. Carry on past the old University College, built in 1867 as the Castle Hotel. In the forecourt is the only public statue in Britain of the future King Edward VIII.

(1277). As you reach the last terraced house of South Marine Terrace on the left hand side, with the harbour in front of you, turn down to the left.

3. Continue along the promenade round Castle Point with its famous 'angel' war memorial, built in the grounds of the ruined Edwardian castle

4. Walk along the road by the side of the harbour 'inner basin', known lo-

cally as 'the Gap', which dries out at low tide. The Vale of Rheidol railway originally ran alongside and terminated here, and cargoes of galena, zinc blende and silver were transferred to small ships in the harbour. Reach the side of Rummers Wine Bar, a former corn warehouse built in 1860, where a Coastal Path waymark sign directs you up steps... at the top turn right, and cross Trefechan Bridge over Afon Rheidol.

5. Once across the bridge look for another Coastal Path waymark sign, which guides you down to the right on the south side of the river.

Turn to the left, past a boat park, and the marina offices on the left. Here

take a block-paved path which edges the south side of the harbour in front of harbour flats to your left. Continue to 'St. David's Wharf', then past the University slipway and clubhouse to arrive at a small tarmac road (Ffordd Pen-yr-Angor) that leads to Tany-bwlch beach.

6. Turn right along this road for a short way, and just before a prominent wartime 'pill box' up on the right, spot a footpath sign pointing

you along a narrow path between privet hedges. The path comes out at the road called Felin-y-Mor, which leads to the Ystwyth Cycle Trail, along the route of a disused railway. Bear right on the road and before getting to the Trail, go through a 'kissing gate' on the left with a signboard for Pen Dinas Local Nature Reserve.

7. Follow the path leading diagonally up the side of the hill, fairly steeply at first with marvellous views back to the

harbour entrance, down to Tanybwlch beach, and below and ahead of you to the Afon Ystwyth winding inland. The path leads round the back of Pen Dinas, even descending a little, before eventually there is an opportunity to turn left, cutting up through scrub to an upper path. Be careful to take the clear and obvious way here, as some 'short-cuts' have been pushed through too soon and are full of gorse and

bramble thorns. The upper path leads left quite steeply to arrive eventually at the 120 m summit.

8. After a well-earned breather, spend time to admire the wonderful 360-degree views and the huge Wellington monument, erected in 1852. In a northerly direction you will see a well defined path leading down... follow this to a small metal gate, then turning

right to descend to a broad bridle track. Just before the first bend in the track you will see a kissing gate in the hedge on the left hand side, go through this onto a path through the trees.

9. Continue down this path until you reach a gate leading onto the main road...A487. Turn left to go past the Street to the Town Clock, then straight ahead again down Pier Street. This will arrive at the pier and promenade.

AND TO KEEP THINGS SAFE & DRY, YOU LEFT THE COMPASS & MAP BACK IN THE CAR.

Terry 2001.

fire station, then reach Trefechan Bridge. After the bridge, you can either retrace your steps via the harbour and Castle Point, or cut the corner off by heading straight up Bridge

Walk 5: Aberystwyth, the Harbour and Tanybwlch Beach. Easy

9 km (6 miles) 3 Hours. Starting point: Grid ref. SN584818.

Starting and finishing at the Tourist Information Centre in Terrace Road, this walk offers varied sea views and a delightful riverside walk along the banks of the Afon Ystwyth. Unusually for the area, the walk is almost level for its whole length with no significant ascents. The route is paved and fairly level along Aberystwyth promenade and by the harbour, then on very well-marked paths and track...there are no stiles. If a car is available, the total distance can be reduced by over 3.5 km (2 miles) by driving to the Tanybwlch car park for the start of the walk.

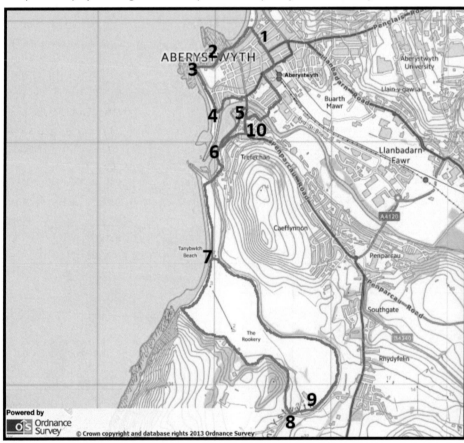

1. From the Tourist Information Centre in Terrace Road, head towards the seafront and turn left along the promenade of Marine Terrace, passing the pier, which was the first in Wales, built in 1865.

2. Carry on past the old University College, built in 1867 as the Castle Hotel. In the forecourt is the only public stat-

26

ue in Britain of the future King Edward VIII.

3. Continue along the promenade round Castle Point with its famous 'angel' war memorial, built in the grounds of the ruined Edwardian castle (1277). As you reach the last terraced house of South Marine Terrace on the left hand side, with the harbour in front of you, turn down to the left.

4. Walk along the road by the side of the harbour 'inner basin', known locally as 'the Gap', which dries out at low tide. The Vale of Rheidol railway originally ran alongside and terminated here, and cargoes of galena, zinc blende and silver were transferred to small ships in the harbour. Reach the side of Rummers Wine Bar, a former corn warehouse built in 1860, where a Coastal Path waymark sign directs you up steps; at the top turn right, and cross Trefechan Bridge over Afon Rheidol.

5. Once across the bridge look for another Coastal Path waymark sign, which guides you down to the right on the south side of the river. Turn to the left, past a boat park, and the marina offices on the left. Here take a block-paved path which edges the south side of the harbour in front of harbour flats to your left. Continue to 'St. David's Wharf', then past the University slipway and clubhouse to arrive at a small tarmac road (Ffordd Pen-yr-Angor) that leads to Tanybwlch beach.

6. Go along this road past the prominent wartime 'pill box' on the right, over the Afon Ystwyth bridge, then turn left at the Tanybwlch beach car park, following the Ceredigion Coastal

Path waymark points along a wide stony track parallel to the beach. Tanybwlch beach is a mostly stony

'storm beach' which feels much wilder and lonelier than the main town beaches. A short concrete causeway or dam halfway along indicates where the river once entered the sea, but now turns sharp right to flow to the harbour entrance.

7. Ahead is the shapely tilted cone of the hill known as 'Allt Wen' (144m) which also forms the sea cliff to the south. Walk to its base, where you turn left through a small metal gate, indicated by a public footpath sign, rather than following the Coastal Path up the steep hill ahead.

Continue along the edge of the flat meadows of the flood plain through another small metal gate, then onto a grassy path which curves round immediately below a mansion called Plas Tanybwlch. Soon after passing a bungalow with its garden, you emerge onto a tarmac lane, which forms the driveway to the mansion, where you turn left.

8. An easy walk on the lane of a little under 1 km takes you round the foot of a steep grassy and partially wooded hill to the right, which was the site of the original Aberystwyth castle, built of timber by the Norman invaders in 1110, and eventually replaced by the stone structure that we see the remains of today on a very different site. This may account for why the town ended up with the name it has, rather than 'Aberrheidol' which may seem more logical. The lane brings you to a T- junction, where you turn left; ahead you will see a kissing gate alongside a field gate next to where the lane turns to cross the river at Pont Tanycastell.

9. Go through the gate to walk the path alongside the Afon Ystwyth, which also offers a dramatic view ahead of Pen Dinas with its Iron Age hill fort (See Walk Number 4). Continue along this to reach the Coastal Path you followed earlier at the point where the river takes its sharp right turn. Retrace your steps to the Tanybwlch car park and the lane alongside the harbour.

ing the bridge, turn right down Glan-rafon Terrace to reach an elegant pedestrian bridge over the Afon Rheidol.

10. For an alternative route back to the starting point, follow the lane to the main road, where you turn left towards Trefechan Bridge. Before cross-

Cross this, go through the car park adjacent to the Aberystwyth Town FC football ground, then emerge onto Park Avenue, with the railway station clocktower over to the left. Take Terrace Road leading to the seafront from the station, to arrive back at the Tourist Information Centre.

Walk 6: The Ceredigion Coastal path: Tanybwlch, Allt Wen and Morfa Bychan.
Hard

13 km (8 miles) about 4 ½ hours. Starting Point: Tourist Information Centre. Grid ref. SN584818

This is an an ideal walk for a clear sunny day because of the stupendous views of sea and hills.   Half the route is along the Ceredigion Coastal Path, heading south. There is a very steep but fairly short climb of 144 m to the summit of Allt Wen, but rewarded all the way up by the wonderful views behind. Otherwise the going is mostly level or downhill, all on well way-marked and dry paths, tracks, and tarmac lane. To reduce the total dis-tance to walk by about 2 miles, drive to the Tanybwlch beach car park at Point 4 on the map.

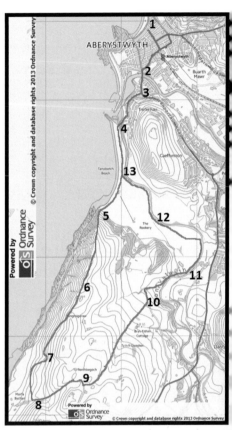

1. From the Tourist Information Cen-tre, proceed down Terrace Road, to-wards the station clocktower, and turn right at the station, straight on past the roundabout then down Mill Street.

2. At the t-junction, turn left over Tre-fechan Bridge over Afon Rheidol.

3. Immediately after the fire station on the right of the main road turn right, taking the tarmac lane which runs along the south side of the harbour. Walk along here for about 600 m, crossing the bridge over the Ystwyth, arriving at the small car park for Tany-bwlch beach. **If you have a car, you can drive to this point and leave your** **car here, instead of the walk from the town.**

4. From the car park, head along the path adjacent to the stony storm beach, or alternatively, take one of the paths along the river side. Walk for over a kilometre, past the point where the river diverts left (point 13 on the map above), arriving at the base of the steep conical hill called

30

Allt Wen.

5. Here, take the waymarked coastal path directly up the hill ahead, keeping clear of the eroded cliff edge to your right. On the steep ascent, you will want to take a breather now and again and admire the tremendous developing view behind, including an unusual angle on the town of Aberystwyth, and Snowdon at 76 km distance.

7. After a somewhat sharp descent in the path, there is a distinctive bend with a gate through to a wide green pasture sloping away to the sea edge. From here, it widens into a grassy track leading along the top of the pasture; round the next bend the Morfa Bychan caravan park comes into view ahead.

6. There is no single clearly defined summit, but the almost constant slope at last eases off and there then follows a delightful undulating walk along the cliff top, with the highest point some way ahead. The way keeps to the right of field boundary fences, gradually descending after the highest point for

After passing through two more gates, follow frequent waymark signs veering left and uphill on an indistinct path to keep above the caravan park, and emerge at a copse of trees onto the tarmac driveway that links the caravan park with the main road.

8. Turn left and go straight up the hill

until the driveway bends sharply to the right. Here spot a waymark indicating straight ahead over a stile into a sheep pasture, where the path is almost invisible. However, the directions of the arrows on the small waymarks are clear enough, the right of way keeping above the lowest point of the small valley to the right, and going steadily uphill. Near the top, bear round to the right, past a scrubby area and emerging over a ladder stile onto a tarmac lane.

9. Turn left onto the lane....it gradually descends with gorgeous views of the surrounding countryside all around. Traffic is very light but be alert for the odd car during the 1 ½ km to a junction with another lane coming in from the right.

10. Turn left in the obvious direction, then after a hairpin bend, admire the neat little church off the lane to the right. In 500 m the lane crosses the Afon Ystwyth at Pont Tan-y-castell, but immediately before the bridge go through a kissing gate onto a river side path. Just before getting to the gate, look over to the left where the closest hill is Tan- y-castell, the site of the first Norman castle in the area, built in timber. It is likely that the name of the town (which arguably should be called 'Aberrheidol') is a left-over from this time!

11. From the bridge, follow the easy flat path alongside the river.

12. Over to the left you will see the large mansion called Plas Tanybwlch which was built by Major General Lewis Davies, a Napoleonic Wars veteran, and at various times used as an isolation hospital, hall of residence, catering college, and rock star's home. In recent times it was converted into luxury apartments, and the encroaching woodland thinned out to provide sunlight on the north-facing hillside.

13. Rejoin the Tanybwlch beach path at point 13 and retrace your steps into town.

Walk 7: Aberystwyth Town Trail

Easy

4 km (2.5 miles) 2 hours. Starting point: Tourist Information Centre

Grid ref. SN584818

Aberystwyth still retains evidence of its medieval castle and town walls. The first Aberystwyth Castle was situated about 2 miles south of the present one at, as the name implies, the mouth of the River Ystwyth. When the present castle and town were established the name was transferred to them even though they were situated at the mouth of the River Rheidol. The building of Aberystwyth castle started in 1277, one of four new castles begun by Edward I after his defeat of Llywelyn ap Gruffudd, part of his plan to encircle the Welsh heartland with towns and fortifications occupied by English settlers; for many years the Welsh were banned from within the walls after curfew. In the mid-18th century the town of Aberystwyth was still confined within the walls of the 13th century borough and to the former Welsh township of Trefechan across the river. The nineteenth and early twentieth centuries saw not only the expansion of the town across the intervening marshy lands towards Penglais Hill, but the shift of the commercial axis from the area immediately outside the castle gate, down Great Darkgate Street, and later along Terrace Road, and also the almost complete rebuilding and infilling of the area within the old walls. The great stimulus from the 1860s onwards was the railway, which enabled Aberystwyth to develop into a seaside town of wider appeal. This 4 km circular walk explores the history of Aberystwyth with particular reference to secular buildings.

1. Leaving the Information Centre turn right and walk to the end of Terrace Road, where it meets Marine Terrace. On your right is a large block of new flats and shops built on the site of the Art Deco styled King's Hall, built in 1934 and for many years a familiar landmark (see nearby information board).

Turn right and walk north along the promenade, to the bandstand which was rebuilt in 2016.

Cross to the promenade. The jetty on your left marks the site of the lifeboat slip built in 1863. The lifeboat used to be hauled on a carriage by horse along the streets from the lifeboat house in Queen's Road to this slip.

Continuing on the promenade, the buildings on your right, on Marine Terrace, comprising hotels and University halls of residence feature stucco and mid-Victorian detailing.

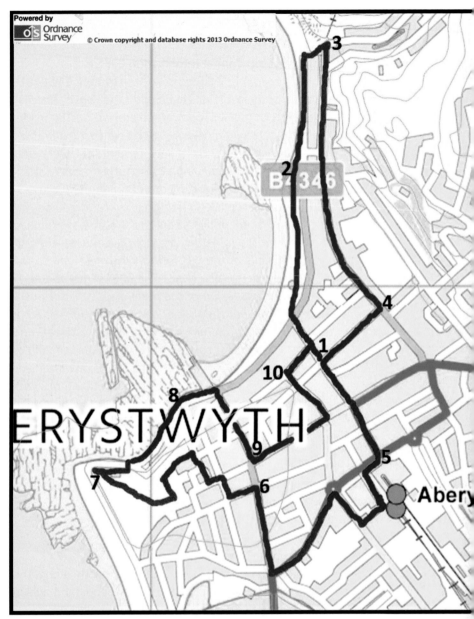

The traditional promenade shelter was restored in 2014 after near destruction by winter storms.

At Albert Place on the right is the former Queen's Hotel of 1866 which was converted post-1945 into Ceredigion County Offices, and is currently destined for a new life as luxury flats. The front entrance, with the addition of a blue lamp, featured as the police station in S4C's acclaimed television crime eries Hinterland (Y Gwyll).

. Continuing on the promenade, beyond the Queen's Hotel, Victoria Terrace breaks the stucco tradition. The next three houses of 1868, and especially Victoria House on the corner, have been painted over, so that their polychrome brickwork is today invisible. Victoria Terrace was continued northwards after 1874.

At the far end of the Promenade is Alexandra Hall, of 1898, built as a women's hall of residence.

after "kicking the bar" (see walk 1) turn right uphill to the bottom station of the Aberystwyth Cliff Railway of 1896. The car bodies are unusual in

having stepped compartments to match steps in the station platforms. Originally operated using the water-balance principle, it was converted to electrical power in 1921.

3. With your back to the station, walk downhill along Bryn y Mor Terrace, then Queen's Road, passing the backs of the Victoria Terrace buildings. Shortly after again passing the former Queens Hotel, the former hotel stables are on the left (now used as car parking for the Marine Hotel).

Continue ahead to Edleston House of 1898 with its two-storey iron veranda made at Coalbrookdale; it was built originally as a nursing home, the first-floor French casements enabling bed

access to the veranda. It has now been converted to luxury flats. Just further on is the converted lifeboat house of ca. 1863.

Further along Queen's Road is the Old Town Hall, now the Town Library. This was rebuilt in 1961 in a neo-Georgian style with thin Adamesque portico and internal full-height entrance hall.

4. Turn right and follow Portland Street to Terrace Road. Turning left, the WHS building (formerly the offices of the Cambrian News) is possibly the finest terracotta building in Aberystwyth.

The junction of Terrace Road and Great Darkgate Street forms Owain Glyndwr Square, formerly Bank Square, and the centre of the present town. Barclays Bank of 1906 has a Portland stone palazzo with curved corner, typical of banks since the 1850s, but with some English Baroque detail to give its actual date away. Opposite, the distinctive white-cladded art-deco style building is a former Burton's store of the 1930s. The building on the other two corners are characteristic Edwardian corner buildings. Tesco's with a spirelet; Siop y Pethe with red brick Dutch gables and a cupola.

Continuing along Terrace Road, the café at no. 20, retains its original mosaic fascia, with "Jukes Draper" in green letters on a gold background. The TSB Bank, further down, is dated 1902 and is of red brick and terracotta, with corner cupola. Cambrian Chambers, of red brick and plentiful terracotta dates from 1902.

At the end of Terrace Road, the railway station is opposite in Alexandra Road. The railway station opened in 1864 the current station frontage being a 1925 rebuild by the Great Western Railway. Part of the building is now a Wetherspoon's public house incorpoating original railway features including ticket windows. The bus station to the left is on the site of the old railway goods yard.

Use the pedestrian crossing and then turn round to view the ca. 1900 group of buildings opposite the station, including the corner building with angle cupola and distinctive semi-circular first-floor windows.

5. At the right-hand side of the station proceed left past a small car park and taxi ranks and turn right across the old school yard to reach Park Avenue next to the public toilets. (continuation past the taxi ranks leads to the Rheidol retail park and the Vale of Rheidol Railway).

Cross Park Avenue to Aberystwyth's most modern architecture, the Tesco

and M&S retail complex. Turn right and pass the old offices of the original town gas works.

Opposite is the Old Welsh School (Yr Hen Ysgol Gymraeg) of 1874, of gothic design with onion-domed roof ventilators, and currently being re-purposed as Aberystwyth's café quarter.

At the mini-roundabout turn left along Mill Street and continue to its junction with Bridge Street. Here on the left is the 1887 Trefechan Bridge over the River Rheidol. Turn right along Bridge Street. On the left, after Powell Street, the white-stuccoed house is Old Bank House, no. 43, once the home of the 1762 Ship Bank. Further on the right, the Old Black Lion pub of 1700 is fronted by a small patch of original cobbled paving.

6. At the corner of Princess Street, Benjamin's is a good example of the combination of terracotta detailing with rough stone, and retains its Victorian shop front. Turn left into Princess Street and then right in St. James's Square past the market hall, originally the 1823 meat market, into Upper Great Darkgate Street. Turn left, go past Castle Street and then turn next right into Laura Place to the Assembly Rooms of 1820.

Walk through the churchyard/car park of St. Michael's Church, then left past

the playground before turning right into the grounds of Aberystwyth Castle. Proceed to the castle headland to the War Memorial of 1923. Designed by Mario Rutelli of Rome, the memorial is crowned by a winged Victory standing on a globe. On the seaward side is a portrayal of Humanity in the form of a naked female emerging from the foliage of war.

7. Descend to the promenade and turn right to pass Aberystwyth University' Old College (Yr Hen Coleg). This began life as a luxury hotel but was purchased in 1867 by the promoters of the University College of Wales, the University being founded in 1872, the first established university in Wales Outside the college building is a rare statue of the later Edward VIII as Prince of Wales (and Chancellor of the University), created by Rutelli in 1922.

8. On the left is the 1865 Pier with its Pavilion of 1896 surviving on the short stub of pier that remains. The pier is the site of seasonal spectacular starling murmurations. Turn right along Pier Street, of late Georgian to Victorian character. No. 38 of ca. 1790 has full

height bow windows and columned porch. The majority of bay windows in Aberystwyth are flat-sided, as a result

of a curious town by-law enacted at the turn of the previous century which insisted that whenever alterations were to be carried out, early-nineteenth-century rounded bays were to be converted to straight-sided bays.

9. At the top end of Pier Street and Great Darkgate Street stood the town hall of 1770, now marked by a clock-tower.
Down Great Darkgate Street, the HSBC

bank building of 1909 shows earlier Welsh origins with the Prince of Wales' Feathers and Welsh Dragon high on the façade. On the right, the old Post Office is a brick and terracotta building of 1901 with its original mosaic fascia. The Santander Bank is on the site of the original Great Darkgate, one of the two main entrances to the walled town. On the corner of Baker Street, the National Westminster Bank, built in 1903, has a façade with 17th-century -style details.

Turn left into Baker Street and walk to the facing old public library. This was a Carnegie foundation built in 1906.

10. Turn right down Corporation Street to Terrace Road. Ceredigion Museum is housed in the old Coliseum Theatre of 1903, which in 1932 was converted into a cinema. It closed in 1977 and opened as a museum in 1983. The building is faced with yellow tiles, unlike the many other buildings with terracotta.

Aberystwyth Ramblers are grateful to the Victorian Society for permission to use their document AN ARCHITECTURAL WALK AROUND ABERYSTWYTH. The document contains much interesting information, including churches and chapels, and is recommended reading. It is available on Ceredigion County Council's website:

http://www.discoverceredigion.co.uk/CCCLocationLibrary/PDF/
Aberystwyth_Architectural_Walk.pdf

or simply search online for Aberystwyth Town Trail

Walk 8: Furnace, Artist's Valley, and views of the Dyfi Estuary.

Moderate

5.5 km (3.5 miles), 2-2 ¼ hours. Starting point: Furnace Car Park on the left before the river bridge on the A487. **Grid ref. SN684952**

This walk offers an eighteenth century charcoal burning iron ore furnace, the best in Wales, a lovely waterfall, spectacular views of the Dyfi estuary and surroundings, and a quick visit to the wooded bottom end of the lovely Cwm Einion, known as 'Artists Valley'. There are no stiles to negotiate, but a fair amount of ascent and descent on paths, tracks and lanes. This classic and popular walk can be taken in either direction. ***Buses X28 or T2 from Aberystwyth will allow you to alight at Furnace.***

1. From the Car park go through the small wooden glade along the track

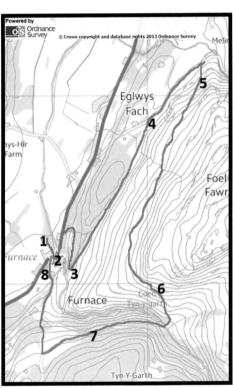

towards the A487. Cross the road taking extreme care, as vehicles appear suddenly over the bridge. Before you is the charcoal burning iron ore furnace which gives the village its name; historical notice boards are strategically placed around the site.

2. From this building go along the A487 carefully, crossing the bridge (looking to the right you will see a beautiful waterfall called Furnace Falls, which

can be approached more closely from the furnace buildings, or via steep paths on the other side of the river). After 100 m, turn right up a lane which ascends steeply, round a hairpin bend,

then becomes enclosed by stone walls covered in moss, reaching a cattle grid.

3. Cross the cattle grid then turn left to follow a path for about 1 km with a stone wall on the left alongside woodland, and the steep flanks of

Foel Fawr (268 m) on your right, until you emerge at a small gate leading into a tarmac lane.

42

4. Turn right to follow the lane for a further ½ km until you reach a kissing gate (beside a farm gate) on your right just before reaching the farm called

Melindwr. Go through, following the path up the grassy slope; this is part of the Wales Coastal Path, and your way rises up the side of Foel Fawr, the low but sharp heathery peak which is so noticeable when driving on the main road.

5. Carry on along this path gently ascending, and at about the highest point, arrive at a viewing place to admire the gorgeous views over Ynys Hir, the Dyfi estuary and beyond. There are particularly good views of the Taren hills across the estuary, which are the southern-most range of the

Snowdonia National Park. After curving round into the bottom end of 'Artist's Valley' (Cwm Einion), the path drops down to a tarmac lane by a waymark post.

6. Turn left, then after a few metres turn right down a track towards Felin-y-Cwm. Keeping right go through a small gate towards the wooden footbridge across Afon Einion, then round to the right and up a path through woodland to another tarmac lane, which is the main Cwm Einion valley lane.

7. Cross over this lane to immediately fork left (you are still on the Coastal

Path) and continue until you reach a junction of paths. Here you turn right down a very rough stony track, then a tarmac lane, to come out on the main A487 road. The track can be slippery after wet weather. (If you want to avoid the stony track continue down the lane to reach the A487).

8. Cross over the main road to arrive at the track back to the Furnace car park.

9. On the way back to Aberystwyth, perhaps stop at the Cletwr Cafe in the village of Tre'r-ddol, a community-run enterprise, for a cup of tea and cake.

7 km (4.5 miles), about 2½ hours. Starting point: Tre'r- ddol. Grid ref. SN660923
The walk starts in the village of Tre'r-ddol which is just off the A487 about 15 km (9 miles) north of Aberystwyth. It climbs through the wooded Cletwr Valley Nature Reserve onto farm land which gives excellent views of the Dyfi Estuary and coastline beyond, then descends passing Bedd Taliesin and old mine workings back to the start.
Park on the roadside in the village or travel by bus X28 from Aberystwyth.

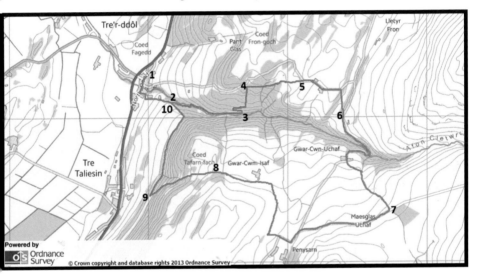

1. From the bus stop near the Wildfowler Inn in the centre of the village walk south along the lane, cross the bridge over the river and turn left just before a disused chapel onto a bridle path, which passes the end of the terrace of houses. This path turns right at the rear of the disused chapel then veers upwards to the left with bungalows on your left.

2. After climbing for about 200 m take the lower level left hand path into the wooded Cletwr valley. Continue along this path, passing a sign for the Wildlife Trust Cwm Cletwr Nature Reserve, until you reach a wooden footbridge on your left. Cross the bridge, taking a moment to admire the flow of the river, then head right along the narrow

path by the side of the river.

3. After about 500 m go through a sturdy wooden gate on your left and climb up the path which slants up the valley side. This levels off, and after about 100 m from the gate take a sharp right turn and continue to climb gradually to another junction, after about 200 m. Turn left at this junction and climb more steeply up this path for about 150 m to take a level path on your right just before the tarmac lane.

4. After about 100 m take the left fork at the white topped waymark post to a stile at the boundary of the Nature Reserve. Cross the stile and continue straight ahead on an indistinct path over rough ground with the fence and

wooded valley close on your right until you see another white topped waymark post. From this post you will see a sleeper bridge over a stream. After crossing the bridge continue straight ahead towards two electricity posts on the skyline. Cross the rough meadow and climb the moderately steep banking to the stile at the base of the first electricity post. At this point take time to enjoy the view down the valley to the sea.

5. Cross the stile and turn right onto a tarmac lane. Continue along the lane past dwellings and farm buildings (Llety lwydin) until you reach a waymarked stile on your right, just before the lane turns left and dips into a shallow valley. Cross the stile and immediately go through the field gate on your left before descending with care on an indistinct path down a rough wooded hillside towards a stile next to an electricity post. Cross the stile and head across the field to another stile which leads to a woodland path which climbs gradually to a tarmac lane.

6. Go through a small gate and turn right onto a tarmac lane which passes a smallholding and descends left back into the Cletwr valley. The lane swings right over a stone bridge and climbs up the side of the valley to a gate in the lane. Go through the gate and turn left before the farm buildings of Gwar-cwm-uchaf on your right and through a gate onto a sunken waymarked track. This passes through another gate and becomes a grassy track which climbs gradually with a stream on your left to a field gate in a stone wall. Enjoy views to the Dyfi hills to the north from this point.

7. Turn right at the gate and head down the stony lane passing Bedd Taliesin on your left (also visited during Walk 10 from Talybont). Continue on the tarmac lane, which turns right through a gate past a farm entrance (Penysarn-ddu). Where the lane then turns left continue straight ahead down the farm track to Gwar-cwm-isaf. The track turns right and after about 500 m reaches a fence and a gate before the track descends left to the farm. Do not go through the gate but turn left with the fence on your right to a stile in the corner of the field. Cross the stile and continue with the fence to your right to join a rough farm track which goes through a gate and heads towards an old mine building.

8. From the mine building continue straight ahead gently downhill across a field to a line of trees. Look carefully along the trees to discover an indistinct track winding its way downhill through the trees to an old mine ruin on your right and spoil heaps on your left. Descend on the rough path between the spoil heaps and the ruined building with a wire fence on your left to a stile at the bottom of the spoil heap. Cross the stile and another stile ahead onto a path which zig zags down

through the woods to meet a broad flat track at the bottom.

9. Turn right and walk along the track which becomes a narrow path with a fence on your left to a path junction. Go through the left hand gate at the junction, down a grassy path and through a gate to meet the path that you started the walk on at Point 2.

10. Retrace your steps to the start of the walk, and perhaps visit the Cletwr Cafe in the village for a cup of tea and cake.

Walk 10: Talybont and Bedd Taliesin   Moderate

7.5 km (5 miles), about 2½ hours. Starting point: Talybont village green.

Grid ref. SN655892

The village of Talybont is at the confluence of the rivers Leri and Ceulan; the A487 through the village bridges both rivers (hence 'bont' meaning 'bridge'). The attractive village, with its two neighbouring pubs on the green, expanded rapidly in the 19th century to house workers in the local lead and silver mines and woollen mills. This circular walk ascends hills to the north-east of Talybont, giving fine views of the village and Dyfi Estuary, visiting Bedd Taliesin (Taliesin's Grave) before gently descending back to the start. The route uses well-signed paths, tracks and lanes, with only one stile.

Park alongside the green or travel by bus X28 from Aberystwyth.

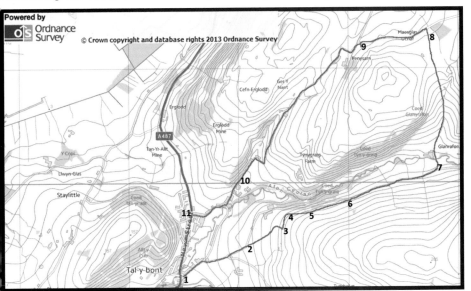

1. Take the lane to the right of the Black Lion pub, pausing at the "Spirit of the Miners" information board next to the public toilets. Follow the lane turning right past the pair of Victorian semis, and after about 200 m take the lane to the left signposted to Nantymoch. In 200 m, where the lane bears left, take a gated track straight ahead.

2. Follow this gently uphill for 300 m to a facing wooden gate. Do not go through the gate, but look for a stile in the stone wall on the immediate left. The stile comprises one protruding step-stone on the near side of the wall and a corresponding protruding step-stone on the far side (look diagonally right when you are on top of the wall). Ascend and descend with care.

3. Walk straight ahead on a track with a fence on your left. After 100 m or so, where the track starts to descend, turn diagonally right gently uphill.

4. The right of way here is indistinct but effectively cuts off the corner of this field. After about 200 m you will converge with a stony track ascending from your left; join it to pass through the gate into the next field.

5. You are now looking up the Ceulan valley. Go straight ahead through the next two fields, resisting any temptation to follow uphill tracks on the right, and exit through a metal gate onto a road.

6. Follow the road for nearly 1 km and take the next lane left to Glanrafon.

7. Passing the farm, follow the gated stony track uphill in a northerly direction for a little over 1 km, until it starts to level out after the third gate.

8. Continue ahead to a metal gate leading onto a lane. Turn left here and follow the gated lane for 700 m in a westerly direction to Bedd Taliesin (Taliesin's Grave), which is in the grass on the left.

9. This is a listed Bronze Age round cairn. According to tradition, Taliesin, the great medieval Welsh poet, grew up in the area. In his old age, he returned to die here, and now lies buried in the hills above the village named after him... 'Tre-Taliesin'.

Leaving the cairn, continue left on the lane, which leads downhill to Talybont. It soon bends to the right then left, and zig-zags once again after nearly 1.5 km.

10. In another 400 m, Penprompen Hall is passed after which the route ahead passes Dol Pistyll and the church to reach the A487.

11. Turn left here to walk through the centre of Talybont, passing several chapels, the old police station which is now the front office of Y Lolfa, the well known printer and publisher, and the garage and a shop, before reaching the village green.

Walk 11: Dyfi National Nature Reserve, Ynyslas dunes and Afon Leri boatyard.

Easy

5.0 km (3 miles), 1.5 hours. Starting point: Ynyslas Turn bus stop, Grid ref SN608925 or Ynyslas dunes car park, Grid ref. SN611941.

The walk starts at the Ynyslas Turn terminus of the 512 bus from Aberystwyth or at the Ynyslas National Nature Reserve beach parking area. It follows the edge of the dunes along the beach and crosses the dunes on a boardwalk, gives the opportunity to call in at the Visitor Centre, passes the Leri boatyard and returns across fields to the starting point. The route gives excellent views across Cardigan Bay to Bardsey Island and the Lleyn Peninsula, the Dyfi Estuary and picturesque Aberdyfi and the hills beyond. Ynyslas dunes and the Dyfi estuary form part of the Dyfi National Nature Reserve. The walk should not be undertaken an hour either side of high tide because the beach section might not be passable at that time.

If travelling by bus, start the walk at Point 1 below. If travelling by car, the starting point is at Point 5.

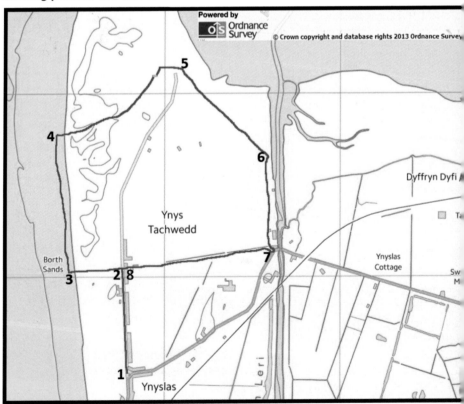

1. From Ynyslas Turn walk with care along the road heading north towards the dunes. After about 500 m pass a group of bungalows and a house on your left and turn left at a gate; a sign warns walkers to look right and left (to avoid flying golf balls) before continuing.

2. From the gate follow a waymarked public path across the golf course. The path emerges onto the beach, providing an excellent vista of the Cardigan Bay coastline and more distant views of Ynys Enlli (Bardsey Island) and the Lleyn Peninsula.

3. Turn right and cross the stones and shingle with care to head north along the edge of the beach. Ignore the first noticeboard and flagpole you will come to, above the shingle. After just over 500 m you will see a second flagpole and waymark post on your right above the shingle at the edge of the beach. The noticeboard at this point warns users of the beach that ordnance, left when the dunes were used as a military firing range during the Second World War, is regularly found at the dunes.

4. Turn right here to leave the beach and follow the waymarked sandy path through the dunes signposted to the Visitor Centre. This sandy path climbs gradually through the dunes to a wooden viewpoint structure and seat. Pause here to enjoy views of the coast, estuary and hills beyond. Continue along the wooden boardwalk which descends gradually to a broken shells path which leads to the Visitor Centre and toilets. Spend time at the Visitor Centre which has interesting information about the dunes and Dyfi National Nature Reserve. Then take the boardwalk path beyond the Centre which leads to the beach parking area.

5. From the beach parking area walk in a south easterly direction along the beach edge past the road entrance to the dunes. Continue in this direction along the edge of the dunes, passing "no entry for vehicles" signs, and a Dyfi National Nature Reserve information board, eventually onto a sandy track. Continue along this track until you see a sign "Private Boat Yard" on your right.

7. At the road, immediately turn right and go through a gate and cattle grid onto a waymarked fenced farm track. Where the track turns sharp left towards the farm, go through the small gate straight ahead and across a field, then through another small gate into a larger field. Follow the line of electric poles to a large gate, then straight ahead to a second gate, passing a derelict concrete building on your right. Walk along a concrete track which passes between a row of bungalows onto the Ynyslas dunes road.

6. Turn right before the sign to head south on a public track with the boatyard on your left. Continue on this track which turns to the left to join the B4353 road at the entrance to the boatyard.

8. If you are travelling by bus, turn left here and walk back along the road to Ynyslas Turn to catch the 512 bus back to Aberystwyth. If you have a car at the beach parking go straight across the road, and then follow Points 2 to 4 above.

Walk 12: Linear walk from Talybont to Borth.　　　Moderate

6.5 km (4.0 miles) 2- 2 ½ hours. Starting point: Talybont.　　Grid ref. SN655892
The walk starts at Talybont village green and finishes at Borth seafront. It follows the waymarked Borth to Devil's Bridge long-distance path, starting by climbing gradually through the Allt y Crib forest west of Talybont, then descending on field paths to Borth. The route gives excellent views of the Cardigan Bay Coast, the Dyfi Estuary, and on a clear day, the Lleyn Peninsula.
Travel on the X28 bus from Aberystwyth to Talybont green and return by train from Borth. Alternatively, return on the 512 bus from Borth.

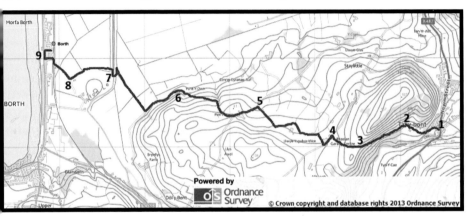

© Crown copyright and database rights 2013 Ordnance Survey

1. From the village green and the two pubs, cross the main A487, and take the lane opposite, heading   towards the Allt y Crib forest. At the end of the lane, enter the forest through a gate.

2. Keeping left follow the track, which is a waymarked bridleway, for about

300 m. Leave the bridleway by taking the waymarked path on your right, crossing a forest track, to continue up a moderately steep path to emerge through a small gate onto open farm land.

3. Follow the field edge with a hedge on left and go through a small gate to stop here for a well earned breather with tremendous views ahead of the Cambrian Coast and bay. Continue down a steepish sloping field with hedge on your left to pass through a field gate and across a second field to the small gate out onto a lane.

4. Turn left onto the lane and walk approximately 200 m going past Rhoslan farm. Find and go through a small gate on the right hand side with two steps up to it. Keeping to the right of the fence this takes you past the farm buildings to cross a stile, then a small gate to the next stile on your left. Cross this stile and take a rather indistinct path keeping to the lefthand edge of the next field. The path crosses another stile and then skirts some farm buildings over to your left, crossing another stile and plank bridge. Head towards the top left hand field corner past the farm, then through a gate and follow a rough track to yet another stile which leads to a large open field. Walk across the field towards the left hand side of a bungalow then along its driveway track to a tarmac lane.

5. Turn left along the lane for about 250 m, ascending gradually past Pen-y- wern farm. Go through a small gate on the right. Keep the fence on your right and continue across a plank bridge and through the next small gate. Continue walking with the fence on your right which veers to the left to follow the path of the pylons and pass through a field gate and down a track onto a tarmac lane past Pant-y-dwn farm.

6. Ahead is a short section which crosses the bottom corner of Cors Fochno, an enormous and important wetland and a National Nature Reserve. Keep on the lane as it skirts the farmhouse for approximately 250 m. On the righthand side of the lane

take the sign-posted kissing gate and follow the path over two successive gated bridges across the section of Cors Fochno.

Turn left here through another kissing gate and onward up the bank pathway to the metal bridge on the right over the River Leri and onto a track.

7. Turn right along the riverside track and after a short distance turn left to progress along a narrow fenced path and cross another gated bridge. Cross the field and pass two stone seats set in the banking. These were donated by Uppingham School to commemorate the evacuation of the whole school to Borth during a typhoid epidemic in 1876-1877.

8. Go through a kissing gate onto a tarmac lane at the beautifully sited St Matthew's Church. Turn right along the lane, cross the level crossing of the main railway line, and continue along the lane to the seafront.

9. If you are returning to Aberystwyth by train, turn right at the seafront promenade and take the next right down to Borth Station. To return by bus, see the bus stop for the number 512 at the top of the road leading to the station.

Walk 13: Linear walk from Borth to Aberystwyth   Hard
on Wales Coast Path.

9 km (5.5 miles), about 3 hours. Starting point: Borth Lifeboat Station.

Grid ref. SN608890

The walk starts at Borth Lifeboat Station and finishes on the seafront at Aberyst-wyth. It follows the waymarked Wales Coast Path which climbs over the spectac-ular cliff-top path to Wallog, with its shingle spit of Sarn Gynfelin, and passes the holiday village at Clarach Bay before descending Constitution Hill to the universi-ty town of Aberystwyth. The route gives panoramic views of the Cardigan Bay coastline and mountains inland.

Travel on the 512 bus from Aberystwyth to Borth Lifeboat Station or on the train from Aberystwyth to Borth.

1. Borth was transformed from a small fishing and seafaring village to a holiday resort when the Cambrian Railway arrived in 1863. Start the walk by heading south from the Lifeboat Station along the seafront road and branch right into Cliff Road which climbs gradually until the road surfacing ends. Pass the wooden sign post (Aberystwyth 5 miles) and go through the wooden gate onto a path between bungalows and the edge of the cliff which climbs more steeply to the war memorial above the cliffs of Craig y Wylfa. Take a breather here to enjoy the views of the northern sweep of Cardigan Bay and on a clear day, the Lleyn Peninsula and Snowdonia.

2. From the memorial descend on a path with a fence on your left and then more steeply down steps into the rocky Aberwennol Bay. Cross a wooden bridge and climb steeply on a zigzag path (ignoring a stile onto private land) onto the headland. From the headland the path ascends more gradually above the sea cliffs, crosses a wooden bridge, and passes alongside gorse bushes to level off to a high point. Take time at this point to enjoy the view back to the war memorial and Borth beyond.

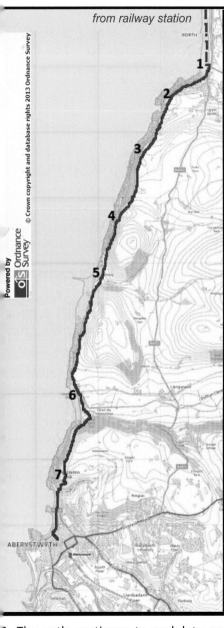

– It's almost perfect", then a deeper

dip to yet another wooden bridge. After the ascent from this dip the shingle spit of Sarn Gynfelin can be seen to the south, depending on the state of the tide. From here views inland to Brynbala farm and the Pumlumon hills can be appreciated.

4. The path now starts its descent to Wallog, gradually at first, then more steeply with the help of steps down to a lower level cliff path which crosses two more bridges and after passing through a wooden gate, continues on a more gradual descent to the bay. This atmospheric part of the walk is a real delight on a sunny day, with a wild, lonely feel to it, and a largely sandy

3. The path continues to undulate on the cliff top, with a dip down to another wooden bridge, passes through a kissing gate immediately followed by a stone with the inscription "John Deans

beach. Go through the gate ahead and cross the stone footbridge then go right on the coast path round the garden wall of the substantial house at Wallog. According to legend, the shingle spit of Sarn Gynfelin, which projects into the sea from here, is an ancient causeway leading to the submerged land of 'Cantre'r Gwaelod'.

The ridge is 20 metres wide and extends out below the surface of the sea for seven miles. According to science it is a glacial moraine left over from the last Ice Age, but that does not detract from its air of mystery!

5. From the house the path continues on the Coast path past a restored limekiln on the beach and climbs gradually onto a low level cliff path. The limekiln, which dates from the early nineteenth century, was used to process coal and limestone unloaded on the beach to

improve acid soils. The cliff path undulates and gives a distant view of the Aberystwyth Old College and Castle, before descending to the Clarach Bay holiday village.

6. Cross the substantial wooden footbridge over Afon Clarach and continue on the seafront road through the village until it turns left and begins to climb out of the village. Take the footpath on the right signposted to Aberystwyth which climbs initially with trees on the left on a cliff path to the summit of Constitution Hill.

7. The summit of Constitution Hill was developed as an early form of theme park when the Cliff Railway was opened in 1896. The attractions remaining include a café, a Victorian style Camera Obscura and a millenni-

um beacon. Walkers can stop at the summit to enjoy superb views of Aberystwyth and Cardigan Bay to the south before descending on the zig zag path which crosses the Cliff Railway twice to the seafront promenade. Walk along the promenade to the bandstand and turn left down Terrace Road to head to the Tourist Information Centre and bus and railway stations.

Walk 14: Rhydypennau and Llandre Circular.   Easy

7 km (4.5 miles) 2-2 ¼ hours. Starting point: The lay-by just beyond the school on the right hand side of the A487, at Rhydypennau. Grid ref. SN629857.

This walk offers country lanes and views towards the coast and Dyfi Estuary, also a historical church in Llandre, with a 2000 year old yew tree growing in the churchyard. There is one stile to cross.

Buses 512, X28 or T2 from Aberystwyth will allow you to alight at a stop opposite the lay-by.

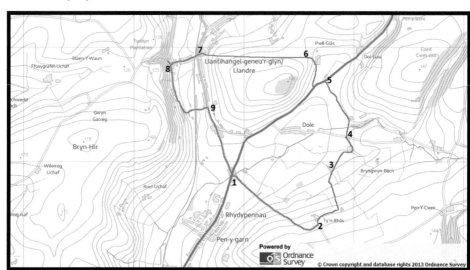

© Crown copyright and database rights 2013 Ordnance Survey

1. From the lay-by walk northwards to pass the Pennau Craft Café and turn

right into a lane,   opposite the road junction to Borth.   Continue up the lane for 1 km, where you should spot a

waymark in the hedge indicating a left turn down a track to pass the farm of Ty'n-rhos.

. Carry on to reach a second gate on he left (way marked). Go through and cross a field diagonally to reach a mall gate in the hedge. Go through to another field, which you cross diago- ally to reach a farm gate just before a mall ford.

. Continue with a hedgerow on your eft to another gate and track leading hrough   Fferm   Bryngwyn   Isaf Frongoch Stud Farm).

after the farm follow the track to cross tarmac lane.

4. Cross the lane to pick up a bridle path, forking left to reach the A487 main road.

5. Cross the road taking extreme care; turn left, then after 100 m right up a bridle path indicated by a waymark in the hedge.

Turn left on the path just before the farm at Pwll-Glas. Continue past sheep pens on your right.

6. Follow this lane at first keeping the hedge on the left , before reaching a gate into a field, where you then keep the hedge on your right. There are good views of the coast from here.

Eventually reach a stile, then descend to a small gate which leads into a tarmac lane at the back of the village of Llandre.

7. Reach the B4353, go straight across and over the railway line, taking extreme care.

Continue a short distance into the village to reach Llandre Church on the right. It is worthwhile exploring around the outside and inside of the church which is normally open. There are also toilets inside at the back. If you have time, try a wander into the woods and follow the 'Poetry Path' around.

8. After passing through the church's lychgate, turn left, to go down the village road, then turn right to go along a lane. At a fork bear left, passing the

Stone Masons, before crossing the railway again. Take care here and please close the gates after you. Continue to the B4353 where you turn right.

9. Arriving at the junction with the A487, turn right to get to the starting point. Perhaps stop at Pennau Crafts for a cup of tea and cake before heading home.

Walk 15: Catch the steam train; Capel Bangor to Aberystwyth.
Moderate

8 km (5 miles), about 2 ½ hours. Starting point: Capel Bangor Station.

Grid Reference SN648797

There are a huge number of walks in the gorgeous Rheidol Valley, and the best way to access them is by using the ever-popular narrow gauge steam trains of the Vale of Rheidol Railway. Detailed descriptions and full illustra-tions for these are given in 'Railway Walks in the Vale of Rheidol', available from the railway shop and the Tourist Information Centre. For this book we suggest a 'linear' route back to town after alighting from the train at Capel Bangor. Although mostly low level and neces-sarily including some semi-industrial suburbs, this walk has an appeal of its own, including lovely views and sections rich with wildlife along the riverbank. Walk-ing is mainly on tarmac lanes, but much of that is a traffic-free cycle path, and there is an optional section of ¾ km on a farm track.

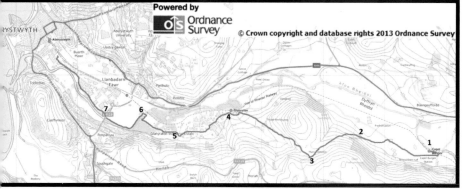

Powered by Ordnance Survey

© Crown copyright and database rights 2013 Ordnance Survey

1. From Capel Bangor station, turn right along the lane heading in a westerly direction. The lane is narrow with raised hedgerows, but with very little

traffic. After just under 1 km, branch left where there is a sign to Pwll-clai cottages. The narrow lane rises gradually up to the houses of Pwll-clai from where there are enviable views for the residents across green and pleasant farm land, the Rheidol river below, with a background of higher distant hills.

2. From here the tarmac disappears, and the track rises more steeply, seriously overgrown from each side with hedgerow in summer, and muddy in winter and after rain. If this seems too daunting to push through, retrace your steps to the original fork in the lanes, and take the surfaced lane close to the railway all the way to Glanyrafon. However, this unpleasant section is very short and it is worth persevering to where the way opens out into high level meadows and beautiful views. The track seems to disappear altogether at a gate, but keep going straight ahead through the gate, then walking to the right of the field boundary. Soon you get to another gate and the reappearance of the track between lines of trees, finally arriving at a hairpin bend on a tarmac lane that descends from the A4120 to Glanyrafon.

3. Descend this pleasant lane past the farm of Troedrhiwlasgrug and meet the original lane from Capel Bangor very close to Glanyrafon Halt. Of course with careful timing, it is possible to catch a 'down' train from here to avoid the suburban part of the walk, but it would also mean missing an interesting section along the riverbank and through Parc-y-llyn.

4. Unfortunately, you must here walk through Glanyrafon industrial estate, keeping in the same general direction, but taking the left turn after about 400 m, signposted towards the recycling centre and cricket pitch. Go straight along this section of road for 500 m, until just past the entrance to the recycling centre there is a gate with a blue cycle trail sign.

. Follow the surfaced cycle path which leads past the sewage treatment works and then via a short patch of woodland to the rather fine town cricket pitch. The cycle trail signs should be followed alongside the pitch then turning sharp right, then left, to arrive at a fine green steel footbridge over the river, with the timber railway bridge nearby.

6. After the steel footbridge, turn sharp left on the cycle trail alongside the river and university sports pitches, then pass under the road bridge carrying the A4120 across the Rheidol (Pont Pen-y-bont)

7. For the next ¾ km through Parc-y-llyn, you can divert left from the cycle trail on well defined footpaths that take you much closer to the riverbank. This is worth doing, to try to spot some of the wildlife (including kingfishers) detailed on the signboards in this nice linear park. All too soon, the paths re-join the tarmac, and you are walking alongside recently built housing and then out onto Boulevarde Saint-Brieuc, (close to the Aberystwyth RFC ground). Follow this towards the town, it becomes Park Avenue, with Aberystwyth Town FC across the road from the Vale of Rheidol station.

Walk 16: Llanon to Llanrhystud Linear Coastal Walk. Easy

4 km (2.5 miles) 1 ½ - 2 hours. Starting point: First bus stop in Llanon.

Grid ref: SN51667

This is a walk between two villages steeped in the history of the land and seafaring. Llanon is named after the church of St. Non the mother of St. David, patron saint of Wales, who was born about 500 A.D. and brought up in the Village. The walk offers country lanes, fields, the Ceredigion Coast Path with lime kilns and historic churches in both villages. There is one stile to negotiate.

Catch the T1 or T5 bus from Aberystwyth bus station, next to the Job Centre and opposite the railway station. Get off at the first bus stop in the village of Llanon. This is about 19 km (12 miles) south along the coast road from Aberystwyth, the next village after passing through Llanrhystud.

1. From the bus stop in Llanon cross the main A487 and walk to a typical 19th century thatched cottage (the property of Ceredigion Museum). On one side of the cottage is a path which leads you around to the village of Llansantffraed. As you walk along this path you will notice on the left narrow field known as 'slangs', narrow strips of farmland for subsistence agriculture...reputedly given to local fishermen by St David himself.

2. Join a tarmac lane, and then you see in front of you the church of St. Brides Llansantffraed, There have been many church buildings on this site since Norman times, the current church dating back to 1838. The unusual south wall is slate cladded, providing protection

against the prevailing south westerly gales that sweep across the slangs of Morfa Esgob. A trip around the gravestones will bear witness to the seafaring traditions of the men from this area.

3. Coming out of the churchyard bear right to reach the Coastal Path; go through two small gates to reach a

grassy track which may be muddy in wet weather, continuing to a field gate. Go through the small gate and along two fields, keeping the hedge on the right. These two fields are very open to the rugged coastline... bird watchers may see migrant pipits, wheatears, wagtails including small flocks of white wagtails in late April, plus red kites, choughs and skylarks.

4. On reaching a third field go through the gate, keeping the hedge on the left before reaching a stile in front of you. Going over this leads you to the Craiglas lime kilns. These were still in operation 100 years ago; lime was hugely valued by farmers far inland to reduce acidity in the soil, thereby in-

creasing fertility, and was brought by boat to many landing sites along the Ceredigion coast. It was also used in lime mortar for building with local shale stone.

5. Passing the lime kilns go over a wooden walkway arriving at a small gate, to continue along the Coastal Path and eventually a stony beach.

(If you do not want to walk on the stones, there is a grassy path at a low-

er level on the right) This will lead you to a tarmac road heading right towards the village of Llanrhystud, with a footpath on the left.

6. Continue on this footpath to reach the main A487 road going through Llanrhystud.

Before catching the T1 or T5 bus back to Aberystwyth, visit the historic church in the village. Its structure dates from 1852, but the lower part of the belfry is thought to have been laid down in the 14 century or earlier.

70

Walk 17: Craig y Pistyll Gorge and Llyn Syfydrin.

Hard

8 km (5 miles) about 3 hours. Starting Point: Llyn Pendam.   Grid ref. SN710839

This is probably the closest walk to Aberystwyth which could be described as 'mountain walking' (at least in part) and is a real favourite. It contains a marvellous contrast of features, including a slightly vertiginous narrow gorge path overlooking the dramatic 'pistyll' (sliding waterfall) , a sense of remote, wild, almost 'wilderness' country, a couple of beautiful lakes, and then later on an easy amble back to the starting point...Walking boots are required and map and compass.

It is necessary to drive to the starting point, which is about 14 km (9 miles) from Aberystwyth. Follow signs through Penrhyncoch village to Pendam. Llyn Pendam is the first of a cluster of small lakes that appears.   There is a small car park amongst the trees on the left, immediately after a t-junction where the road gets close to one end of the dam. This is the starting point of our walk

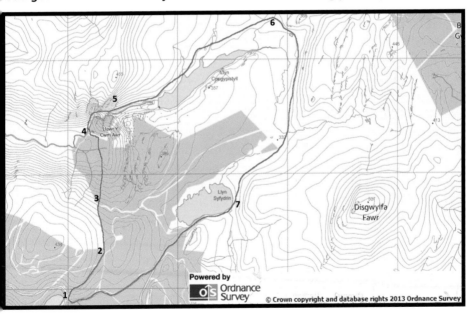

1.   There are numerous mountain-biking trails in this forest, so it is important to find the footpath rather than following one of those. Go up the bank at the north side of the car park, avoiding the more obvious mountain-biking trails over to the right. The way-marked footpath climbs diagonally be-tween the trees, with glimpses here and there towards Llyn Blaenmelindwr and the more distant mound of Disgwylfa Fawr (507 m).   Which views you get depend on the cycle of cutting and planting of the fast-growing conifers. The attractive path leads northeast-wards for 500 m, and then drops down

to join the broad stony track used by cyclists to get to the same point.

2. Here, bear left off the track immediately to pick up a footpath running north along the edge of the forest with open hillside to the left. The start of this path is wide and has wooden barriers to prevent use by motorised trail bikes, but it rapidly becomes narrow alongside the fence, eventually descending, with views of the sea and parts of the Lleyn Peninsular appearing over to the left. The path drops very sharply down to a forestry track, which we cross straight over and continue our descent steeply through forest.

3. Following the yellow arrow waymarks, we next emerge into a more open area of forest plantation. Gradually a wonderful view straight ahead appears of the rugged south side of Pen Craigypistyll (455 m), a real 'miniature mountain' whose smoothly curved plunging profile is easily seen from the whole Aberystwyth area.

Walk in the direction of the yellow arrows on the waymarks; what you will see around you depends on the stage of growth of the fast-growing trees. Pass a much-ruined building on your right, and then the steep descent levels out onto the flat valley floor.

Cross a sturdy footbridge over a small stream, following the path and way marks carefully. Keep going to where the plantation ends at a grassy fire break in front of the mature forest ahead. Here the path turns left towards a small isolated cottage at Llaw y Cwm Awr. The public right of way passes near the cottage, and is sign posted towards a very substantial timber footbridge across a rushing mountain stream. This stream is the upper reach of the Afon Leri, which flows via Tal-y-bont into the Dyfi estuary at Yny -las.

4. The footbridge makes a very good first stopping point. From here. notice above and to your right the clearly defined but narrow footpath which ascends diagonally overlooking the Leri gorge on the steep flanks of the mountain. It looks formidable and risky, but with a little care can be walked easily and we must first attain its bottom end

by struggling up to it over small ridges in the ground, bearing slightly right until we hit the obvious ascending path. Now we will be walking steeply uphill with looming crags above us, and an increasingly high and steep drop down to the river gorge to our right.

The only slightly tricky bit of the path is towards the top where it skirts some screes and becomes, briefly, very steep and a little loose underfoot. This is where you are glad to have such good grippy soles on your boots!

After rain, particularly, the obvious sight and sound will be the dramatic narrow waterfall, the 'pistyll'...the Afon Leri shooting down the smoothed rocks of the gorge...

5. All too soon, the path begins to level off and the landscape starts changing dramatically. A short walk brings you to the dam of Llyn Craigypistyll, a water supply reservoir. From hereabouts there is the option of a climb to the summit of Pen Craigypistyll alongside the fence you will see on the skyline or on the rather hair-raising path just visible rising diagonally across its face. As this is designated 'Access Land', leaving the public right of way is legal, but the drawback is the thick tussocky grass, gorse, and heather that makes the ascent very tiring. You will be rewarded at the summit with a fabulous view all round, followed by a quick return to the dam. Continuing on the path alongside the lake, the landscape has a 'wilderness' feel to it. The lake has an austere beauty, and the path is easy to follow on the ground in good weather. In mist, rain or snow, it is essential to use map and compass effectively on this part of the walk.

6. The path eventually arrives at a 'meeting of the ways' where you cross a ford on the stony track, then turn

right at the t-junction of tracks and start heading in a south easterly direction. Very soon you pass the isolated ruined farmhouse of Bwlchystyllen, which always seems to have a haunting, sad, beauty; you wonder what dreams died when the house was abandoned...Continue on the same track for almost 2 km, avoiding getting wet feet in the standing water which always seems to dominate here, but look up often enough to admire the wild country around Disgwylfa Fawr. The way here is mainly level or slightly descending, so although a bit of a 'route-march' it is very pleasant for all that, with wide views; eventually Llyn Syfydrin comes fully into view. On a fine day, this lake is picturesque and sparkling, edged with forest and lots of ideal shoreline picnic spots.

kilometre along this road winding through pleasant forest, you arrive back at the starting car park on your right.

"I think this next section is down-hill".

7. From being a rough track earlier on, the going becomes a surfaced lane across Llyn Syfydrin's dam, and beyond. After leaving the lake behind, follow the lane uphill through forest, and take the right fork when you get to a hairpin bend on a slightly wider surfaced mountain road. Walking another

Walk 18: Ascent of Pumlumon Fawr (752 m) via Maesnant

Hard

7.5 km (4.5 miles), 380m (1240 feet) ascent, 3 - 4 hours.
Starting Point: Maesnant.   **Grid ref. SN775879**

Walking in the Aberystwyth area is perhaps not complete without the ascent of the local mountain, Pumlumon Fawr, and a taste of this exceptionally wild-feeling country so near at hand. The 'normal' route up from Eisteddfa Gurig is only popular because of its easy access from the A44, but the north and west sides are far more interesting and give a much more scenic walk. The crags of the northern cwm of Llyn Llygad Rheidol are only seen from this walk, and give a quite different perspective of the mountain. The route, unusually for Pumlumon, is for the most part fairly dry underfoot, but for some of the way only faint foot-paths are available to follow. **Private transport is required to get to the starting point...take the mountain road signposted to Nantymoch from Ponterwyd. Soon after spotting the large concrete dam over to your left, take a right turn at a t-junction up the eastern arm of the lake, until the tiny surfaced lane final-ly ends at a gate and turning point at Maesnant. Park in one of the off-road areas nearby.**

Please note that walking boots, map, and compass are needed for this walk, as well as adequate waterproofs. Wind, cloud, rain and snow can be severe on the mountain, even when it is fine weather in Aberystwyth.

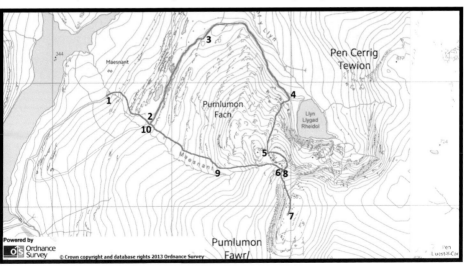

1. The stream called Maesnant can be crossed on a very rickety wooden foot-bridge and a faint path is followed straight up the very steep grassy slope, well to the left of the stream in its gulley. The gradient soon levels off, the

path heading across an area of bleak bogginess, before threading its way between rocky outcrops and beside small waterfalls. Persevere up this first section, jumping across the stream at one point, then picking the driest way across a level but very boggy area, before emerging onto a stony track which crosses our path. All the really wet sections are now over; unfortunately this first part is repeated at the end of the walk!

2. Turn left onto the relatively dry, level track, and look around as you walk

to enjoy the wonderful mountain scenery from this higher level. Behind are the broad stretches of the Nantymoch reservoir, its far bank rising steeply to the 550 m summit of Drosgol. Ahead

and to the left is Banc Llechwedd-mawr, and straight ahead the valley of Cwm Hyddgen. Pass a series of pools on your left, with the shapeless bulk of Pumlumon Fach on your right.

3. At the third main pool, the track starts to bend round to the right, and

even descends a little, but not much height is lost, and you are soon facing into the dark ring of crags overlooking the cwm and small glacial lake of Llyn Llygad Rheidol, the source of the River Rheidol. To the left is Pen Cerrig Tewion (677 m). The summit of Pumlumon Fawr is still invisible ahead and to the right, and the waters of

the small lake are not seen until you are up close to it.

4. You will notice that this small lake is actually a reservoir with a dam, although there was a glacial lake here already when the dam was built. It is just about possible to drive a motor-

ised vehicle right up to this point, and unfortunately some people do, at some cost to their suspensions and clutches. But now the slightly wearisome 2 km 'route march' is over and the real ascent begins; stop on the track at the very last left hand bend

just before the dam is reached. Look carefully and you will see faint paths leading off the track to the right. They

soon join forces and lead slightly right avoiding a small outcrop, and then the path bears left straight up a steep but shallow grassy gulley, with a scree

slope to your right. Notice the shapely pointed crag above; at first you should be heading almost directly towards it if you are on the correct route. Follow the faint path carefully, climbing rapidly with good views of the small lake behind you, the gradient easing very

slightly as you pass to the right of the shapely crag, and ascend towards the skyline with Pumlumon Fach on your right.

5. With the slope distinctly levelling off now and approaching the 'bwlch' at

around 650 m height, you have the option to take an even fainter path left which rises up over a knobbly outlying peak at 668 m. This gives good views

down towards the north crags of the mountain and the small lake below. Drop down the other side to another 'bwlch', where you head to the right (west) for a short distance. Alternatively, keep going straight on and join a more well-defined path which winds left round the base of the small outlying peak and very soon arrives at the bottom of the main ascent onto the Pumlumon ridge.

and as you ascend steeply, you usually start feeling the full force of the westerly wind for the first time! Keeping the steep western scree face on your right, the gradient eases onto a shoulder then steepens again, but eventually you will see a large cairn over to your left, and a smaller one marking the path you are on. Ahead is the trig point and summit shelter.

7. Take your time to admire the wonderful panorama from the top of Pumlumon Fawr! A distinctive feature

6. Taking either route, spot an isolated large boulder which marks the beginning of the path leading up to the summit. This path is quite clearly defined,

is the dark plunging profile of Craig y Pistyll to the west, and the town and coastline beyond. Heading back towards the large cairn, on a clear day you will see Aran Fawddwy in the far distance ahead. Near the cairn, branch left to pick up the path you came up on. Descend to the bwlch between the main mountain and Pumlumon Fach, arriving at the "marker" boulder once more.

8. After the boulder go straight ahead, but very soon notice a diverging path, branching off to the left which seems

to cut off a corner in the main path and then rejoin it further down. This is somewhat boggy after rain, so it may be best not to take this diversion. Either way, don't go right on the path you came up, but go left on the more distinct path down the side of the shallow gulley formed by the Maesnant stream on the western side of Pumlumon Fach.

9. Follow the path with the Maesnant stream well over to the left and slightly below you, your way gradually curving rightwards, heading down towards the eastern arm of Nantymoch reservoir. As you descend, negotiate a few short steep inclines in the path and some boggy patches. At each area of wet soft ground, walkers have picked their own individual way through and the path seems to disappear.

10. Eventually reach the stony track from the beginning of the walk...Go straight across it, and immediately splosh carefree through standing water and bog. Pick up the path, jumping across the stream, and retrace your steps from the beginning of the walk back to your waiting vehicle.

Walk 19: Bwlch Nant-yr-arian Visitor Centre; Circular via Llechwedd Gwinau (optional extension to Llyn Blaen melindwr)
Easy/Moderate

6 km (4 miles), 1 ½ - 2hours. Starting point: Bwlch Nant-yr-arian Visitor Centre. Optional extension adds up to 3 km (2 miles)   **Grid ref. SN718813**

*A gorgeous high level walk with stunning views, well-maintained dry path throughout, and easy wayfinding. The route follows the Natural Resources Wales' waymarked RED walkers' route starting and finishing at the NRW Visitor Centre. The optional extension taking a loop round Llyn Blaenmelindwr is mostly on quiet tarmac mountain roads. **The Centre is adjacent to the layby where the A44 main road reaches its first highest point, about 10 miles from Aberystwyth.***

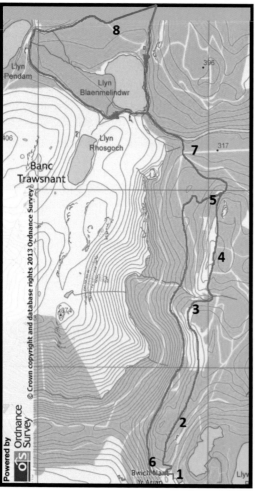

1. From the Visitor Centre car park, take the small path to be seen zig-zagging up the steep hillside, ascending quickly with lovely views to the right and behind, and following the red way mark arrows. The only complication on the entire walk is the extensive network of well signposted mountain-biking trails which occasionally cross you walkers' path, and are to be avoided.

2. You will soon arrive at the 'giant's chair' on which children (and others) like to climb. The

gradient has eased off at this point, and along the path are various seats, viewpoints and picnic tables from which you can now also admire the view westwards towards the sea and, in the far distance, the 'Wellington Memorial' on the summit of Pen Dinas.

3. Keep going along this lovely high level path until at about 1 km from the

start, the path makes a meandering descent to a bridge over a small stream and then a short sharp ascent up the other side.

4. The highest point ahead is at about 385 m altitude (1,250 feet) from which

you begin to gradually descend on a widening stony track through the for-

est. This winds downhill, getting steeper and into denser woodland, until you get to a fork in the track where you must decide whether to follow the red marker for the return to the start, or if you wish to extend the walk to Llyn Blaenmelindwr, keep right following the waymark for the Borth to Devil's Bridge to Pontrhyd-fendigaid long distance path. (Go to Point 7 below)

5. For the shorter option, the red waymarked path continues to wind through lovely forest, emerging onto a somewhat lower level path where you turn left to head back to the Visi-

tor Centre. This path rises gently at first, and then after a dip and footbridge for the previously-encountered stream, soon becomes quite a spectacular ledge-path (formerly a mine leat) with wonderful views of the parallel valleys to the right. A little bit of care is needed, particularly with children, but this path is generally fine even for those without much of a head for heights.

6. A final rise over the shoulder of the hill at the end brings you back to the car park and Visitor Centre, near where you can see the feeding of the red kites every afternoon.

7. To carry on to Llyn Blaenmelindwr, follow the track down through the forest and emerge where several tracks meet in the clearing. Turn to the right, then very soon turn left on a tiny tarmac road uphill which switchbacks up to the highest point, from where you will see the lake ahead. Turn left at the lakeside on the road, following it round for about 1 km until next to the dam for Llyn Pendam there is a T junction where you turn right.

8. Follow the lane to a hairpin right turn which then leads back to Llyn Blaenmelindwr. Retrace your steps keeping right to where your track emerged from the forest. Keep right here, and you will join the path described in Point 5 above.

Walk 20: A railway walk; Devil's Bridge to Rhiwfron Halt.

[The Pine Marten Trail: information at the station]   Easy/Moderate

3 km (2 miles), about 1 hour. Starting Point: Devil's Bridge station.

Grid Reference SN738769

The walk is wonderfully scenic, with lovely views down to the upper Rheidol valley. The path is steep and slippery in places with a steep uphill climb at the end. There are frequent waymarks throughout.

Take the Vale of Rheidol steam train from Aberystwyth to its Devil's Bridge terminus, and catch the same train returning, at Rhiwfron Halt.

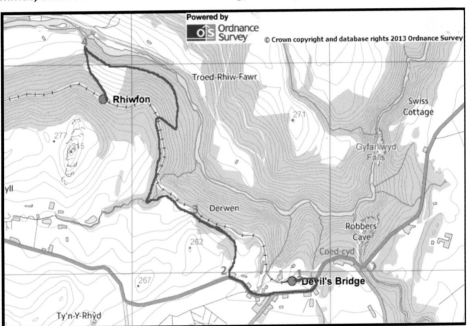

Powered by Ordnance Survey © Crown copyright and database rights 2013 Ordnance Survey

direction. Be careful of traffic, particularly in the holiday season. As you pass the last houses of the village on your right, a footpath sign is reached on the right-hand side.

This is on a left hand rising bend, and rather indistinct.

2. Go through the gate into the meadow, looking for a waymark post straight ahead of you. The path is not very clearly defined here, but follow

1. From the station, turn right on the main A4120 road and walk about 500 m along the road in the Aberystwyth

83

the direction of the waymark arrows, soon bearing gradually round to the left. You are on a long-distance path from Borth to Devil's Bridge, and the waymarks have a characteristic design. Look out for the chain of further waymark posts and signs to follow; very soon the path becomes much clearer, undulating through the woods, and the railway is seen below you to the right.

3. A sharp, craggy zig-zag descent in the path leads you out onto open meadowland by the railway, and now you have to look out for waymark posts to follow in order to find the way as the path is again indistinct. The arrows point you round uphill beside the trees and then round to the left and down into the wooded gulley of Nant Fawnog. You cross the stream on a good footbridge; there is a small

waterfall and a nice little glade, followed by the path rising to the right again. A little further on the clear path overlooks the railway, with good views into the valley, and a seat! You then

descend to cross the railway, approximately 20 minutes after the start of your walk. After crossing, the path descends steeply to the right, then left again through the forest on a long straight descent, with the sound of the river below getting louder. The path eventually levels off and then even rises again slightly, finally reaching a gate, stile and signboard where a fine view opens out ahead of you to the west down the valley.

4. You need to allow 20 minutes for the last section, the steep climb up to the Halt. You are close to the river here, but now turn left, cutting back on yourself sharply on quite a small path climbing and zig-zagging steeply up through the forest; take care. A little way up the hill and after some slippery sections of narrow path, you meet a wider bridle path ascending in roughly the same direction. There is still quite a long pull up before you arrive at the eastern end of Rhiwfron Halt.

Walk 21: A gorge walk at the Hafod estate.

Moderate

5 km (3 miles) 1 ½ - 2hours. Starting point: Hafod estate car park.

Grid ref. SN76873

A book of walks in the Aberystwyth area would not be complete without visiting the Hafod estate near Cwmystwyth.. This was the 18th century property of Thomas Johnes, who built a mansion and the extensive grounds designed by John Nash in the fashionable style of the times...known as 'Picturesque'. This also involved creating scenic walks, many of which are still available for our enjoyment today although the mansion is long gone. The estate is owned by Natural Resources Wales, and jointly managed with the Hafod Trust. Today the area feels like a natural landscape, is mostly wooded, with entrancing streams, waterfalls and bridges, and there are a multitude of possible walking routes, several of which are waymarked with a colour-coding. The walk chosen for this book visits three

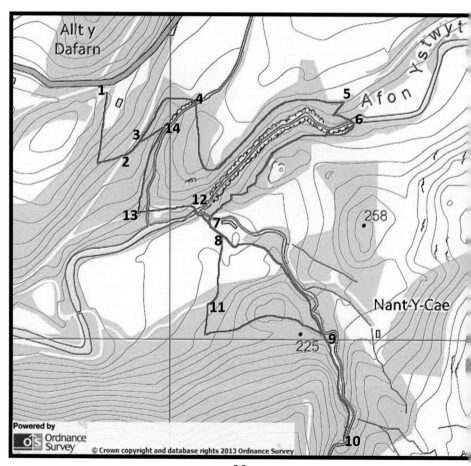

gorges, and several waterfalls and delightful footbridges, and is mostly on broad, easy paths, except for the slightly narrower, steeper path up to the 'not-to-be-missed... Cavern Cascade'. **Catching the T22 bus towards Cwmystwyth would get you to within 2 km of the start of the walk, but it is easier to access by car...from Devil's Bridge take the road towards Cwmystwyth, and just before the village, follow the signposted lane to Hafod. Spot the Upper Lodge on the left, a little further on there is a small car park with information point, near the estate church.**

1. The information board here details a range of colour-coded walks which would suit a range of ambitions. To begin our gorge walk, follow the yellow, blue and green arrows from the car park, taking the wide descending path through the forest with the church below to the left. Ignore the yellow arrow off to the right just before the gate leading into the churchyard, and keep on descending steadily

down through the trees. Resist any temptation to cut off the corner, but very soon the main path zig-zags down left, and continues across an unmade lane, following the blue and green arrows.

2. Very soon there is a fork in the paths, the one to take is the higher level to the left, following the green arrow.

3. Keep going along an easy, wide, very slightly ascending path, noticing the attractive falls down in the gorge to the right, which we will see close up on our return. Soon you will find the path curving to the right to cross the gorge above the falls via a newish wooden footbridge (the old path crossed higher up on another bridge you will see upstream).

4. After the bridge the very wide path ascends at first then descends gently, soon curving left, cut out from the solid rock when the original landscaping was undertaken. The easy path continues through the forest, still following the green waymark arrows.

5. Eventually there is an abrupt and slightly awkward hairpin bend right, the path suddenly going down much more steeply, and then another zig-zag left descending towards another footbridge, this time a wobbly plank and rope construction across the deep cut

gorge of Afon Ystwyth. Despite its appearance, this bridge feels reassuringly safe but fun to cross, and anyone on it can be photographed from a vantage point a little further on.

6. The path, now narrower, bends to the right and goes up above the gorge, towards a triple arch 'folly' from where good photos of people on the 'wobbly' bridge can be taken. From there, fol-

low the path up through the forest again ascending a long series of wide "sleeper" steps before dropping again down the other side of the hill, winding down between trees to arrive at the wooden footbridge over Nant Gau at Dologau.

7. There is an attractive series of torrents and an old stone arch bridge to admire here, and a gate through to a track where we see the green arrow pointing right, and the red arrow indicating straight on. Here we turn left on the track, ignoring the waymarks, then almost immediately go to the right where there is a choice of directions.

8. The track then curves to the left with an open field on the right hand side. Very soon look out for a waymark post with a red arrow indicating left towards the hedgerow, amongst which you will find a stile leading in to an open meadow. Go uphill close to

the edge of this meadow, with nice views down the valley, and at the top arrive at another stile offering access back into forest. Here there are large boulders; a good place for a sit down! Keep going ahead, slightly left, keeping close to the stream, following a narrowish path winding up through the wooded gorge.

9. Spot a sign pointing in the direction of the 'Cavern Cascade' (Lefel

Lampwll), and head up, the path rising and winding uphill, keeping the stream over to the left and below. At a fork, where a path descends to the stream and a footbridge, there is a red waymark arrow to follow indicating your route straight ahead. Spot waterfalls on the main stream, Nant Gau, and further on a very attractive fall of a smaller stream coming in from the left. There is also a mine level cavern to pass on the right of the path. You are now nearly at what is marked on the OS Map as *'Grotto'*. The path gets steep and rocky, and then finally a short steep but easy scramble arrives at the mouth of a second cavern, this one offering an exciting 'Wow' experience. Go carefully and slowly here, into the dark cavern, whose floor is uneven and always has deep puddles. Feeling the cavern wall, ease your way forward towards the roaring sound you can hear. The cavern bends round to the left and arrives at the cascade, a truly stunning sight and sound amid a fine spray of cold water, even in the driest and warmest summer.

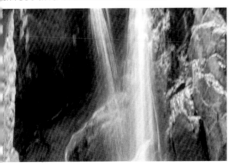

10. Retrace your steps from the 'Cavern Cascade' back down the gorge path for approximately 300 m to where you will see a footbridge below to the right across the stream, (see point 9). Here there is a waymark with a red arrow pointing to the right and also another red arrow indicating straight on up the hill. Go straight on, ascending, and very soon see another post with two red arrows, one indicating a 'viewpoint' option. Either of these will do... where there is a choice head right, and eventually go downhill on a broad path towards the edge of the forest and the open field encountered at Point 8 above.

11. Join the track at the field edge and arrive back at Dologau with its bridges...the one to cross this time is straight ahead across the Afon Ystwyth.

12. Bear left on the wide track, passing a few holiday cottages, until you get to a blue waymark arrow pointing up a path on the right leading off the track.

13. This path leads uphill and arrives at the base of the first waterfall spotted on the walk. At the waterfall, the path turns left more steeply ascending and joins your original path from point 2 above. Retrace your steps on the 'green' route, first crossing the vehicular lane, then zig-zagging up the hill towards the church and car park. The church is well worth a visit at the end of your walk, and has its own information boards for visitors. The far gate of the churchyard leads onto the road along which you approached the car park on arrival.